A Way other than Our Own

Devotions for Lent

Walter Brueggemann

Compiled by Richard Floyd

WJK WESTMINSTER
JOHN KNOX PRESS
LOUISVILLE • KENTUCKY

© 2017 Walter Brueggemann

First edition
Published by Westminster John Knox Press
Louisville, Kentucky

17 18 19 20 21 22 23 24 25 26—10 9 8 7 6 5 4 3 2 1

Unless otherwise indicated, Scripture quotations are from the New Revised Standard Version of the Bible, copyright © 1989 by the Division of Christian Education of the National Council of the Churches of Christ in the U.S.A., and are used by permission.

Some content has been previously published in Walter Brueggemann, *The Collected Sermons of Walter Brueggemann*, vols. 1 and 2 (Louisville, KY: Westminster John Knox Press, 2011, 2015) and is used by permission.

Book design by Sharon Adams
Cover design by Eric Walljasper

Library of Congress Cataloging-in-Publication Data

Names: Brueggemann, Walter, author. | Floyd, Richard A., editor.
Title: A way other than our own : devotions for Lent / Walter Brueggemann ; compiled by Richard Floyd.
Description: Louisville, KY : Westminster John Knox Press, [2017]
Identifiers: LCCN 2016032960 (print) | LCCN 2016036187 (ebook) | ISBN 9780664261696 (pbk. : alk. paper) | ISBN 9781611647877 (ebook)
Subjects: LCSH: Lent--Meditations.
Classification: LCC BV85 .B74 2017 (print) | LCC BV85 (ebook) | DDC 242/.34--dc23
LC record available at https://lccn.loc.gov/2016032960

♾ The paper used in this publication meets the minimum requirements of the American National Standard for Information Sciences—Permanence of Paper for Printed Library Materials, ANSI Z39.48-1992.

Most Westminster John Knox Press books are available at special quantity discounts when purchased in bulk by corporations, organizations, and special-interest groups. For more information, please e-mail SpecialSales@wjkbooks.com.

Contents

Compiler's Note

Prolonged exposure to Walter's work performs a kind of alchemy on the soul, gradually transforming our cramped and sclerotic vision into something more capacious and generous. He is an excellent, if occasionally disruptive, companion for the Lenten journey.

Walter's incisive exploration of Scripture reveals the same prophetic message found in Isaiah and Jeremiah calling to us also through the Psalms, Torah, gospels, and even a handful of epistles. We are invited to walk a Lenten path that may be barely recognizable to our self-indulgent and violent world—a path marked by grace, compassion, and abundance.

Those of us who were students of Walter will recall the arresting prayers with which he began classes. I have tried to draw on his language in constructing the prayers, and hopefully some small measure of his spirit.

Richard Floyd

An Old Identity Made New

Seek the LORD while he may be found,
  call upon him while he is near;
let the wicked forsake their way,
  and the unrighteous their thoughts;
let them return to the LORD, that he may have
  mercy on them,
  and to our God, for he will abundantly pardon.
                                                —Isaiah 55:6–7

These verses are a familiar call to worship or a call to repentance, not a bad accent for Lent. The face of God shown here is of a Lord near at hand, ready to forgive, *a God of grace*. But this is a God to whom a turn must be made, *a God of demand*, a God of demand ready to be a God of grace . . . not just hard demand, not just easy grace, but grace and demand, the way all serious relationships work.

The imperative is around four verbs, "seek, call, forsake, return," good Lenten verbs. But this is not about generic repentance for generic sin. I believe, rather, the sin addressed concerns for Jews too eager to become Babylonians, too easy to compromise Jewish identity, Jewish faith, Jewish discipline—in order to get along in a Babylonian empire that had faith in other gods with other disciplines. The imperatives are summons to come back to an original identity, an elemental discipline, a primal faith.

I suggest, moreover, that these are just about the right imperatives for Lent among us Christians. For I believe

2

the crisis in the U.S. church has almost nothing to do with being liberal or conservative; it has everything to do with giving up on the faith and discipline of our Christian baptism and settling for a common, generic U.S. identity that is part patriotism, part consumerism, part violence, and part affluence.

The good news for the church is that nobody, liberal or conservative, has high ground. The hard news is that the Lenten prerequisite for mercy and pardon is to ponder again the initial identity of baptism . . . "child of the promise," . . . "to live a life worthy of our calling," worthy of our calling in the face of false patriotism; overheated consumerism; easy, conventional violence; and limitless acquisitiveness. Since these forces and seductions are all around us, we have much to ponder in Lent about our baptismal identity.

Lent is a time to consider again our easy, conventional compromises and see again about discipline, obedience, and glad identity. And the climax of these verses:

> that he may have mercy . . .
> for he will abundantly pardon.
> Isa. 55:7

The word to the compromised deportees is that God's face of pardon and mercy is turned exactly to the ones who reengage an identity of faith.

> *God of grace and demand, you challenge us to reclaim our baptismal identity as those whose lives are built on your call and your promises—not on the easy, seductive forces around us. Stir our hearts that we may engage your transforming word anew and rediscover its power to save. Amen.*

On the Road Again

I lift up my eyes to the hills—
    from where will my help come?
My help comes from the LORD,
    who made heaven and earth.
                              —Psalm 121:1–2

We are on the road again! As followers of Jesus, we are on the road again in Lent, walking the way of obedience to Jerusalem for the big showdown with the authorities of church and state. It turns out, every time, to be a hazardous journey, full of toils and snares, potholes and adversaries, ending in a rigged trial. But women and men of faith are always on the road again, departing safe places, running risks, and hoping for well-being on the journey.

The defining journey of biblical faith begins in the departure of Abraham and Sarah back in the book of Genesis. They were dispatched by God to leave their safe place, to go to a new land yet to be given, to get a new name, to be blessed by God, and to be a blessing to the others around them. They went! And their family, generation after generation, has gone. And we, finally in their wake, must also travel beyond safe places to the gifted end that God intends, hopefully to be blessed and a blessing on the way.

And if we ponder our destination, perhaps it is to be to the neighborhood of *shalom*, the neighborhood of shared resources, of inclusive politics, of random acts of hospitality and intentional acts of justice, of fearless neighborliness that is not propelled by greed or anxiety or excessive self-preoccupation.

Psalm 121 is designed exactly for travelers who face a demanding, risky journey. It is a psalm that has been used over and over by travelers and now is available for us. This psalm is an assurance and an affirmation that the journey we now undertake is not by ourselves alone. We are surrounded on the way by the God of all trust, the God who kept Abraham and Sarah safely, the one who walked all the way to Jerusalem with Jesus, all the way to Friday and on through to Sunday.

I imagine Lent for you and for me as a great departure from the greedy, anxious antineighborliness of our economy, a great departure from our exclusionary politics that fears the other, a great departure from self-indulgent consumerism that devours creation. And then an arrival in a new neighborhood, because it is a gift to be simple, it is a gift to be free; it is a gift to come down where we ought to be.

> *Self-giving God, call us to walk the road of*
> *newness—a new self, a new society, a new world,*
> *one neighbor at a time. May we have traveling*
> *mercies this Lenten season. Amen.*

A New Way of Being in the World

> And can any of you by worrying add a single
> hour to your span of life?
> —Matthew 6:27

L ent is a time when we ask about the meaning of
repentance. Lent could be a time not when we think
about all the sin and suffering and self-denial that have
been traditional with us, but when we ask in fresh ways
what the people clustered around Jesus make of the world
they are in. I put the question this way: Jesus affirmed that
it is possible to be in the world in a new way, to be present
to the people and problems around us with some newness
and freshness.

The usual way of being in the world is anxiety, of being
pressed and harried and worried, and that in turn leads to
a stance of defensiveness and fear and a determination to
keep what we have. Anxiety that believes that we best get
what we can and keep what we got snowballs on us, and
we get caught up in it and don't know it's happening.

Characteristically, Jesus asks a question which doesn't
require an answer because it's so obvious. It is a question
which just stops all our protests and explanations short.
You know it well: Which of you, by being anxious, has
ever added an inch to your lives?

I find that a biting, embarrassing question, because of
course, it is true. Being defensive and frightened and cov-
eting has never really resulted in any gains. Partly we do it

6

because we don't know any better way and partly because it's habit. In either case, he suggests another way:

Seek the kingdom and his righteousness.

Put another way:

Get your mind off yourself long enough to care; be so concerned about the well-being of the human community that you don't have to worry about your place, your church, your class, your values, your vested interests.

Now this could be a sermon on emotional well-being that says quit worrying, but that is hardly what Lent is about. Rather—this is a talk about the mission of the church. The invitation is to get so involved in the emergence of humanness, human persons in all their delicacy, human institutions in all their effectiveness, human relationships in all their mystery, humanness, wholeness, that we don't have to be defending how it was, worried about what will happen to the things to which we have given our lives.

Free us, Lord, from our obsession with ourselves
long enough to care for others; to be so concerned
about the well-being of the human community
that we don't have to worry about our place, our
church, our class, our values, our vested interests.
Help us to know the joy and freedom of putting all
our trust in you. Amen.

A Trip, a Temptation, a Text

> Jesus, full of the Holy Spirit, returned from the Jordan and was led by the Spirit in the wilderness, where for forty days he was tempted by the devil.
>
> —Luke 4:1–2a

So we are on the way in this business of Lent. There is *the assuring voice* of God, which says, "I will protect and I will answer and I will deliver." That voice, however, is countered by a *second voice* that mocks and seduces men and women of faith, making easy promises, issuing facile invitations, urging acts that are against our faith and our identity. Lent is a time for learning how to listen to the voices of promise and seduction and decide how to adjudicate them, to hear better the true voice of assurance and to notice quickly the seductive voice of unfaith, and to distinguish the same psalm when it speaks faith and when it serves unfaith.

It will be a gain for us to see our Lent as placing us between these conflicting voices. Christians in our society are cast exactly between these voices epistemologically, deciding if we have faith that seeks understanding or if our learning is simply power packaged as knowledge. Christians in our society are cast between these voices in terms of political and economic power, to see whether we can honor the pain-filled voices of marginality or if we will notice only the tired claims of the old monopolies.

Christians in our society are cast between these voices in terms of self-identity, to see if we can receive the innocence of real faith or if we will practice the old cynicism of despair, which works most of the time. We are at risk because the very assurances of God can be turned against our true selves as a warrant for cheap, self-serving actions.

We begin our Lenten journey addressed by the remarkable assurance that the God who summons us is the God who goes along with us. We begin our journey knowing we will want to ease off and not take the risk. We will have chances, epistemologically, economically, in terms of self-perception, to make decisions, hearing more than one inviting voice. The world thinks this journey is unimportant and therefore easy. Well, yes, the world may think it easy, because it is only faith that requires entering the danger zone where our lives are at risk.

> *Teach us in this season how to listen to the voices*
> *of promise and seduction and how to tell them*
> *apart. May we hear better your voice of assurance*
> *and recognize its counterfeit, that we may walk*
> *faithfully before you. Amen.*

Lent as Alternative to Empire

Ho, everyone who thirsts,
　　come to the waters;
and you that have no money,
　　come, buy and eat!
Come, buy wine and milk
　　without money and without price.
Why do you spend your money for that which
　　　is not bread,
　　and your labor for that which does not satisfy?
　　　　　　　　　　　　—Isaiah 55:1–2a

S ome of you will remember these TV ads from AT&T.
They featured a winsome young teacher or librar-
ian sitting at a table with young children. He engaged
them in friendly talk through a series of questions. The
questions of course led to the conclusion that we should
buy AT&T products. But the teaching addressed to the
viewer through the children was this: it is better to do two
things at once rather than only one thing at a time. Bigger
is better. Faster is better. More is better.

This poem of Isaiah is a wake-up call for us when
we have been nearly talked out of faith by the force of
empire, when we have wanted to prevail instead of trust
mercy, when we have decided to gut it out rather than let
the pardon come, when we have bought in to the phoniness of the AT&T ad rather than the God of the gospel
who gives free gifts.

Lent is a question, a gift, and a summons.
The questions of Lent are:

What are we doing?
Are we working for that which does not satisfy?
Are we spending for that which is not bread?

The gifts of Lent are free, gifts in the gospel that sustain life: free wine and milk, free water and bread, and all the markings of sacrament that refuse our thin attempts at empire.

The summons of Lent is to bear new fruit. Do what is in sync with the God of the gospel, the God who has another intention for our lives, who wants us out of the rat-race of "big is better" and so has mercy, who gives us pardon when we do not do enough by doing two things at once.

We are left with a new sense of ourselves as God's people:

no longer working for that which does not satisfy;
receiving good gifts that we need for life;
engaging in a new productivity of that which heals
    and transforms.

This could be, for any one of us, a return to our true self after almost being talked out of it.

You are the God who disrupts our lives with an invitation. During this season of Lent, may we stop and may we start again: may we stop our strivings marked by greed and anxiety, may we start again the work of compassion and generosity. Amen.

Habits That Make God Unhappy

> But God chose what is foolish in the world to
> shame the wise; God chose what is weak in the
> world to shame the strong; God chose what is
> low and despised in the world, things that are
> not, to reduce to nothing things that are, so that
> no one might boast in the presence of God.
> —1 Corinthians 1:27–29

The cross is a contradiction to the world and pertains to public policy just as it pertains to personal well-being. The cross exposes the way of the world in a fantasy land where we hunger for that which cannot satisfy. The cross—with its death and its odd Easter victory—asserts that the self-serving of the world in its self-confidence cannot prevail.

There are escape hatches to this type of subversion, which is so risky. One is to throw over this claim in secularism and get a day job that will bring it all home in power, wealth, and wisdom. The other is to keep the form of Jesus but to turn the truth of weak, foolish poverty into a worldly force. The first temptation is that of those outside the church. The second is the temptation of those inside the church. Either way, the truth of the gospel compels us to decide about the things that make God unhappy and the things that make God happy. Because God is God, there are habits of death and there are habits of life.

Wouldn't it be something if all the conservatives among

us would get honest in the company of the church and confess, "I would rather not delight in the things of God!" And
wouldn't it be something if all the liberals would get honest
and confess, "I would rather not delight in the things of
God!" What an energy and a newness if liberals and conservatives together would make cause together, that we do not
want to choose the hard way but must decide to anyway.

And then Paul grows lyrical:

> God chose what *is foolish* to show the wise little acts
> of compassion that violate our learning.
> God chose what *is low and despised* in the world to
> reduce to nothing the things that are low and
> despised, in the form of Jesus of Nazareth, and the
> rulers of the world are not finished with him yet.

Folks, the odds are always long. But entertain this:

> the world waits for newness;
> *settled wisdom* knows nothing of newness;
> *settled wealth* knows nothing of newness;
> *settled power* knows nothing of newness.

But we do, and so we consider our call and occasionally
choose what makes God happy. Take an instant today
and brag a little: Brag that you know the things in which
God delights. Celebrate that you delight in that which
makes God most happy.

> *You have ordained a new order in which the first
> are last and the last are first. Turn us away from
> the false values of the world, that we may pursue
> your priorities, that which makes you happy:
> steadfast love, justice, and righteousness. Amen.*

On Terms other than Our Own

> And he said, "I will make all my goodness pass
> before you, and will proclaim before you the
> name, 'The LORD'; and I will be gracious to
> whom I will be gracious, and will show mercy on
> whom I will show mercy."
>
> —Exodus 33:19

The story of Exodus 33 is about an awkward, complex negotiation with the future. God is cranky and absolute. Moses is defeated but is not willing to sacrifice the community just because God is upset. And therefore Moses bargains, trying to figure out the limit of God's responsiveness. That is what we do when we are fresh from failure. We find out what is possible in a new start.

God is *gracious*. God is assuring and affirming and generous and kind. God is *merciful*. God has compassion and empathy and a readiness to be available in decisive ways. God is gracious, and God is merciful. And that is what Moses most hopes for, for the new journey after the big failure; the future after failure depends on God's graciousness and God's mercy.

But there is a catch. It is that this pronouncement does not say simply that God is gracious and God is merciful. Rather, God is gracious toward those whom God wants to be gracious; God is merciful toward those whom God wants to have mercy on. It is all on God's terms. Hard bargainer that he is, Moses now is able to discern that the true God upon whom the future depends is not a good luck charm or a nice, kind uncle or patsy. The future is on God's terms, and it will not be otherwise. Israel is expected to give up all of its pet projects of religion, all of its favorite convictions, all of its conservative ideology, all of its liberal propensity, to notice that God has not signed on for any of our easy preferences.

Moses learns what people of faith always learn:

> the future beyond failure depends completely on God and not us;
> God's way is a way of graciousness and mercy;
> but it is grace and mercy on God's terms, not ours.

We receive from God only hints and traces, and we must be very suspicious of those who claim to have God and know God and speak for God.

We people of faith do not have life on our terms. And we, like Moses, have to decide that we will walk into the future on terms other than our own.

> *Irascible God, you offer us a future full of grace and mercy, but on your terms, not ours. Knowing that you go with us into this future, may we respond with thanks and praise. Amen.*

Flooded with Fidelity

> God said, "This is the sign of the covenant that I make between me and you and every living creature that is with you, for all future generations: I have set my bow in the clouds, and it shall be a sign of the covenant between me and the earth. When I bring clouds over the earth and the bow is seen in the clouds, I will remember my covenant that is between me and you and every living creature of all flesh; and the waters shall never again become a flood to destroy all flesh.
> —Genesis 9:12–15

This is not about water. It is about God. It is about the God who emotes in anger but who circles back with a second effort to flood us with fidelity. And because it is about God, it is about us. And because it is about us, it is about you . . . and me. It is about the world being flooded with fidelity that is the divine antidote to the craziness all around us. It is a witness to God's second effort, God's new sanity after a moment of divine craziness. It is an invitation to respond with sanity to our present special craziness.

So consider:

we are flooded with the gifts of neighborliness—the economy of the rich devouring the poor is now inappropriate;

we are now flooded with peaceable possibility—the
    old lust for war and violence is now out of sync;
we are flooded with fruitfulness—the technological
    destruction that seeks to sustain our unsustain-
    able standard of living is now passé.

God does not here demand that we stop the craziness
in which we are presently enmeshed. But God's great second effort makes our present craziness inappropriate, out
of sync, and passé. The rainbow is aimed at God. But it
would not hurt if we noticed it as well, as a reminder of
the ocean of fidelity in which we live our lives:

we are left dazzled by a God who has made a new
    resolve about creation;
we are left aware enough to notice the regularity of
    gift-giving creation;
we are left grateful that God gives and gives and gives,
    in keeping with God's own pledge of fidelity.

Imagine what it was like that day, to step off the ark
into a peaceable land. And now the work is toward a new
life that matches God's new promise. It is our proper
work. We are inundated by God's loyalty. God remem-
bers . . . and so we may not forget.

Remembering God, hold before us this Lenten
season the promise of your commitment to creation.
Flooded by your fidelity, may we work toward a
new life that matches your promise. Amen.

Summoned beyond Ourselves

Then Jesus answered her, "Woman, great is
your faith! Let it be done for you as you wish."
And her daughter was healed instantly.
                                        —Matthew 15:28

Jesus reached beyond his people, beyond his perceived
mandate, beyond his tradition, extending himself to
the "other." Notice that something powerful happens to
Jesus in this narrative because the woman is persistent.
She is *the outsider* who instructs *the insider*. She explains
to Jesus his larger vocation that he had not yet embraced.
He is willing, in turn, to be instructed by her. In the narrative, we can watch while Jesus rethinks his vocation and
his mandate as Messiah. He learns that full faithfulness
means reaching beyond one's comfort zone to care for
the other. He now, in a new way, enacts the *gathering of
humanity*.

I believe this is the big issue for us in our coming world.
All of us, to some extent, hold the line against "the other."
All of us, to some extent, know that our faith calls us out
beyond that. Some of us are more able and more willing to
enter the risk of inclusiveness, to embrace the others who
threaten us. It is clear in these texts that the good news of
God's love and God's healing and God's justice cannot be
kept just for us and people like us. I imagine that by the
end of the story Jesus thought to himself, "I never antici-
pated that I would be instructed by a Canaanite woman

18

to reach beyond myself." But the pull of God's largeness summons all of us, often through the words and presence of "the other." The old teaching of exclusion cannot fully protect us from God's pull to be a neighbor. We are neighbors to foreigners and to eunuchs and to mothers of tormented children who yearn for healing. God calls us out beyond our comfort zones to be surprised by the fact that "her daughter was healed instantly."

> *Gathering God, draw us out beyond our cramped*
> *circles of care. Draw us toward the neighbor,*
> *the other, the outsider, the hurting one. May we*
> *practice compassion. Amen.*

First Sadness, Then Gladness

> "Blessed are you who weep now,
>   for you will laugh."
> . . . .
> "Woe to you who are laughing now,
>   for you will mourn and weep."
> —Luke 6:21b, 25b

In his "woe," Jesus reviews the "laugh now" party. The "laugh now" party consists of those who celebrate the way things are, who benefit from the way things are. The "laugh now" party is filled with buoyancy and confidence, looks extremely well fed, speaks only positively, and sleeps unhindered at night.

Jesus says of the "laugh now" sect: "You will mourn and weep." You will have your laughter silenced. You will plunge into grief when the bubble bursts, as it surely will. You will face loss, because the close reasoning of Jewish control will not last and because the Empire of Rome, like every empire, will pass away soon. And you will be left bereft.

Moaning and grieving and weeping have to do with relinquishment, about which we are always reluctant. I think, speaking to that point, that the church's struggle about welcoming gays and lesbians is not much about sexuality. It is about clinging to an old world we could manage wherein we felt safe. We always fight a rearguard action against relinquishment: if not gays, then Muslims,

and if not Muslims, then immigrants, and after immigrants we will find new candidates around whom to draw
a line against relinquishment. It is a common temptation
among conservatives and among liberals, for nobody I
know wants readily to give up what we treasure.

Laugh later! It is an Easter laugh. It is a laugh when
all the powers of death—that come in the form of greed,
violence, anxiety, exploitation—have been defeated. The
church is that body of disciples who have relinquished
enough of that old world of death—that is, greed, violence, anxiety, exploitation—that we can watch and
notice the coming of God's new rule that is an Easter
arrangement.

What if the church is the place in town that refuses to
participate in the "laugh now" movement of buoyancy,
prosperity, and sureness? What if the church becomes
the venue for processing loss and acknowledging grief for
a world that is gone? It is precisely such processing of
grief that permits hope.

> *Strengthen us to relinquish the old world, O God,*
> *that we might receive the gift of hope and joy on*
> *the other side of grief. Amen.*

A Vision That Dis-Comforts

> In the year that King Uzziah died, I saw the
> Lord sitting on a throne, high and lofty; and the
> hem of his robe filled the temple. Seraphs were
> in attendance above him. . . . And one called to
> another and said:
>> "Holy, holy, holy is the LORD of hosts;
>> the whole earth is full of his glory."
>>> —Isaiah 6:1–2a, 3

It is to be taken seriously that the genre of this pas-
sage is theophany—*vision of God*. That is, its complete
strangeness must be respected and not explained away.
The preacher must not try to make the meeting familiar
to us. Its substance is the *Holy God*, who is never familiar
to us. Its mode of expression is poetry, myth, image, fantasy, vision, dream. It is a moment of fleeting clarity that
comes always as a surprise if it comes at all, a moment not
given on demand, in which everything is now seen afresh
and radically. In this vision comes a word that redefines
Israel, a word that *jeopardizes and reprimands*. That is, it is
a word of heaven given *to judge the earth*. The Holy God
is not an easy mark, but it summons Israel to *look and listen
and hear and turn* . . . which it will not do.

In the book of Isaiah, it is now suggested that 6:1–8
is matched by 40:1–11, a second meeting of Yahweh's
"divine council" that gives a second message, one of *well-
being and comfort*. As 6:1–8 offers the theme of *judgment*

in chapters 1–39, so 40:1–11 voices the theme of *comfort* expressed in chapters 40–66. The two themes are held in tension, likely correlating 6:1–8 and *Good Friday* and 40:1–11 as the *Easter* of the book of Isaiah. Both are there. But Friday comes severely before Sunday, and so we attend to the hard vision first. God's holiness puts us in danger. This text is indeed a mouthful, possible and bearable only when it is recognized that in this utterance, the real King comes near.

> *Holy God, you come to us as one unfamiliar . . .*
> *the power of your presence overturns all our*
> *expectations. May we hear and receive your word*
> *of danger, that we may also receive your word of*
> *comfort. Amen.*

Like a Thief in the Night

> Now the LORD came and stood there, calling
> as before, "Samuel! Samuel!" And Samuel said,
> "Speak, for your servant is listening."
> —1 Samuel 3:10

There is an odd turn in the tale of the boy Samuel. The action takes place at night. He is lying down. The lamps in the temple are burning. Now admittedly, we do not come to church much at night, and if we do, it is usually for something other than meeting this holy God.

But imagine! Like the boy Samuel, our real meetings are at night, if we take "night" to be a metaphor for "down time." Night is a time when we cannot see. Night is when we cannot control. Night is when children are frightened, because the shadows seem lively. Night is when things are unclear and beyond explanation. Night is when we are terrorized, and so we have bright lights all around the house to fend off the darkness. Night is when even adults are out of control, and we are visited by our haunted past and our feared future, and we dream and have nightmares. . . .

The nighttime is bewildering. The boy did not understand, and the old priest was slow to figure it out. It was bewildering to him because something not routine was happening. The anthropologists call this "liminality," an unsettling feeling at the threshold of something new, when life is gathered into a wholly new configuration.

Now I say this because too often the church in our

society is thought to be a place of unambiguous answers and sure certitudes, where we come settled and cocksure, and the spirit has no chance to change anything. Liberals get it all settled, and conservatives get it all settled. It is, however, more often than not, nighttime in the church—bewilderment, confusion, liminality, unsettlement. Then emerges something new from God that comes like a thief in the night.

The narrative suggests that the holy place must not be understood with too much daytime certitude, but with something more like nighttime bewilderment. For it is in such odd moments that we sort out the voices of address, and God works the newness of nurture and vocation, demand, and promise and healing. So think of this place, as did the boy Samuel, as a place of the nighttime, when new voices utter our names.

> *Divine thief in the night, you come to us in the darkness to unsettle our expectations and certainties. Open our hearts to bewilderment, that we may be open to your wisdom. Amen.*

Seeing Clearly, Loving Dearly, Following Nearly

"One thing I do know, that though I was blind, now I see."

—John 9:25b

The confrontation between the authorities and the man who can now see is a dramatic one. It is a contrast between *old established truth* that keeps everything in place that has all the answers, that keeps everything under control and assures certain entitlements, and on the other hand *new inexplicable possibility* by Jesus and eventually by his people.

So imagine us as participants in this great drama. Standing before Jesus is the one with new life who worships him and the defenders of old truth who refuse him. They each and all must decide about Jesus. It turns out that seeing is to accept Jesus and blindness is to refuse him.

And now we stand before the new chance of gospel possibility and old managed truth. Old managed truth, like the rule on the Sabbath, takes many forms. It can be the old world of privilege and power and control. It can be the old truth of settled church orthodoxy. It can be the old mantras of market ideology that reduce life to owning and having and eating. It can be the old paralysis of privilege according to race, class, gender. It can be an old image given you by your mother or your father that has kept you from the freedom and joy of God's love.

And over against all of that old managed truth is this

26

man who testified to new bodily possibility because Jesus has moved him into a new life that he did not even expect for himself. Jesus is an invitation and a chance and a summons to a different way of life. And we are always deciding.

And we worship and give thanks and obey and bear witness. We say, I am the one who was blind. I have no explanation, but I received my sight. We see more clearly; then we love more dearly the one who gives sight. And then we follow more nearly, giving sight to others. Clearly, dearly, nearly. This does not make the old authorities happy; but it is the truth of our life.

> *You are the God who unleashes well-being into the world. May we see; may we love; may we follow. Amen.*

True Self-Denial

> He called the crowd with his disciples, and said
> to them, "If any want to become my followers,
> let them deny themselves and take up their cross
> and follow me. For those who want to save their
> life will lose it, and those who lose their life for
> my sake, and for the sake of the gospel, will save
> it. For what will it profit them to gain the whole
> world and forfeit their life?"
>
> —Mark 8:34–36

Jesus' words are stark and starchy. *Let them deny themselves.* The saying is loaded and dangerous and has often
been misunderstood. In more pietistic and moralistic
church traditions, it is often understood as saying "no" to
something you really want a lot, of foregoing something
you deeply enjoy—like giving up ice cream for Lent, or
meat on Fridays, or movies on Sundays . . . perhaps not
in themselves bad disciplines, but not the point of Jesus'
saying. The call to discipleship is not a program to make
us feel bad or impoverished or uncomfortable. Or pressed
more deeply, to deny self is taken too often to mean you
should have some self-hate, feel bad about yourself, ponder your failure and your guilt, and reject your worth. But
that is surely not what Jesus is talking about.

Rather, he is talking about coming to see that God—
the generous creator who gives good gifts—is the center
of your life and that the self-taken-alone does not have

28

the resources or capacity to make a good life. To deny self means to recognize that I cannot be a self-starter, cannot be self-sufficient, cannot be self-made or self-securing, and that to try to do so will end in isolation and fear and greed and brutality and finally in violence. It will not work because we are not made that way. It will not work even if all the consumer ads tell us to have life for ourselves. You cannot have the life you want that way.

The alternative to self-focus is to move one's attention away from self to know that our life is safely and well held by God, who loves us more than we love ourselves, to relish the generosity of God and so to be free of the anxieties and needs and hungers of those who are driven by a mistaken, inadequate sense of self. The self who is denied is the self who is received from God and given back to God in obedience and praise.

> *God at the center of our lives, our true life is found only in you. May we let go of all that is not life, all that is not you, that we may live in that freedom granted through the cross. Amen.*

Neighbor Religion

Is not this the fast that I choose:
　　to loose the bonds of injustice,
　　to undo the thongs of the yoke,
　to let the oppressed go free,
　　and to break every yoke?
　　　　　　　　—Isaiah 58:6

Lent is the time for cold, sober reflection on that which our faith knows that we have mostly forgotten. The God of the Bible so wants human community to work, right here. But the God of the Bible also tells us what it costs for community to work. What it costs is a harsh criticism of the terrible advantage some have over others. God is indeed "pro-life," for the poor, for the hungry, for the homeless, for the naked. When these become the center of policy, the city becomes both pro-God and pro-life.

Isaiah's poem concludes with these poignant words:

Then your light shall break forth like the dawn,
　　and your healing shall spring up quickly;
your vindicator shall go before you,
　　the glory of the LORD shall be your rear guard.
Then you shall call, and the LORD will answer;
　　you shall cry for help, and he will say, Here I am.
　　　　　　　　Isa. 58:8–9

"Then," when you have done true religion, light will come. Healing will surge. There will be a healing of fear and hate and brutality. "Then" your righteousness will be established. You will soar in success and safety, in splendor and well-being. Then, and not before. Then, and not without this costly caring.

Then you will cry out and God will answer. God will be with you, full of promise, genuine community, right blessing, a safe people. The condition of such blessing and presence, however, is the condition of justice for all those too weak to have it on their own.

The promise of God is for here and for now and for you. That promise, however, allows no short-cut, no light for the city without the fast of genuine humanness. The fast of humanness is the condition of Easter, when all God's children in this place come to new life. Imagine, entrusted to people like us—entrusted with true religion, invited to true economics, destined for true community—is a new city, brilliant in its light, powerful in its common faith, beloved in its shared humanity. The light is promised to us. The fast is required of us.

> *Save us, Lord, from a religion that ignores the cries of the exploited and oppressed. Lead us into a deeper faith that challenges injustice and makes the sacrifices that must be made to build a society that is ever more truly human. Amen.*

Caught by God

Surely goodness and mercy shall follow me
　all the days of my life,
and I shall dwell in the house of the LORD
　my whole life long.

—Psalm 23:6

"Goodness and mercy pursue me." God's friendliness and kindness will run after me and chase me down, grab me, and hold me. The verb "follow" is a powerful, active verb. We are being chased by God's powerful love. We run from it. We try to escape. We fear that goodness, because then we are no longer in control. We do not trust such a generosity, and we think our own best efforts are better than God's mercy.

Lent is a time to quit running, to let ourselves be caught and embraced in love, like a sheep with safe pasture, like a traveler offered rich and unexpected food. Our life is not willed by God to be an endless anxiety. It is, rather, meant to be an embrace, but that entails being caught by God.

The second concluding line is, "I shall dwell in the house of the Lord forever," that is, "my whole life long." I will hang around the church. Or I will live in attentive communion with God. I will not depart from the premises of God's life, because I have no desire for a life apart from God. Why would I want to leave? Now you may think such a conclusion is sweet and unreal, or at least something only for old, tired people who don't get around much anymore.

To the contrary. This conclusion is the reflection of a mature life, when one "comes down where you ought to be." The last line of the psalm asserts that the true joy and purpose of life are to love God and be loved by God, no longer alone, but in communion. Our anti-Lent society gives us many desires. These, however, will never constitute a good life. The matter has been settled in the first line for this poet. This sheep community trusts God and wants nothing else.

Lent is about noticing our blindness and seeing differently. I invite you, during this Lent, to see differently, maybe even for the first time. To see past your anxiety, your greed, your fear, your control. See yourself as the sheep of this Good Shepherd, as the traveler in God's good valley, as the citizen at home in God's good house. You will, when you see truly, be free and joyous and generous, unencumbered and grateful. Desire one thing: God's presence. And you will be less driven by all those phony desires that matter not at all.

> *Pursue and catch us, Good Shepherd—embrace us in your love. Help us to trust you and desire you more than anything else, that we may know the joy and freedom of life in you. Amen.*

Third Friday of Lent

A Nighttime Gnaw and a New Possibility

> Now there was a Pharisee named Nicodemus, a leader of the Jews. He came to Jesus by night and said to him, "Rabbi, we know that you are a teacher who has come from God; for no one can do these signs that you do apart from the presence of God."
>
> —John 3:1–2

We have this dramatic meeting between Nicodemus and Jesus. Maybe he went to see Jesus out of curiosity. But likely this was more, because it was a huge public relations risk to make the night venture. I suspect that Nicodemus—lawyer, scholar, politician, CEO, whatever he was—had a gnawing concern that made him climb into his limousine and seek out Jesus. He had everything, and he wondered, "Is that all there is? Is there something more? Is there something different? Am I on the right track?" Well, what would motivate a big-time public winner to such a secret meeting? It must have been a *gnaw* about reality.

Jesus knows this is no idle curiosity. And so like a good therapist, Jesus hones in on Nicodemus, disregards his dossier and his portfolio and reaches toward his gnawing sense of deficiency. Jesus says to him: "You've got to start over! You've got to be reborn. You've got to be born again. You've got to be born from above. You've got to become as vulnerable and innocent and dependent as a little child. You've got to forego your social position, your achievements, your wealth, your reputation. You've got to let go of all the things that make you self-sufficient and that alienate you from the wonder of the gift of God. *Start over* in *vulnerability*, in *innocence*, and in *dependence*, for the way you are living now keeps you cut off—in your arrogant security—from all the gifts of life for which you so much yearn."

What a perfect text for Lent. Because many of us stand alongside Nicodemus in our bewilderment and in our urging and in our gnawing. Like Nicodemus, honor the gnaw in your life. Go. Seek.

When the secret meeting is over, Nicodemus gets back in his limo and rides back to the city. He has work to do. But he leaves with these odd words pounding in his head:

> For God so loved the world that he gave his only Son, so that everyone who believes in him may not perish but have eternal life. (v. 16)

Nicodemus understood this was no easy mantra. It was, rather, an invitation to be reborn—*innocent, vulnerable, dependent*—open to the *wind*, fixed on the one with *the cross*. He found his world had been opened and his old world contradicted. He wondered, "How could this be?" He wondered whether his old self would be turned to new self. And we, alongside him, also wonder.

> *In this season of Lent, O God, unsettle us. Increase in us that sense of gnawing that arises from the incongruity between our lives and the life to which you call us, and transform us in newness. Amen.*

Power for Life Flown in by Bird

> The word of the LORD came to [Elijah], say-
> ing, "Go from here and turn eastward, and hide
> yourself by the Wadi Cherith, which is east of
> the Jordan. You shall drink from the wadi, and I
> have commanded the ravens to feed you there."
> —1 Kings 17:2–4

This is a story about the oddness of Elijah. Elijah is
shown to have the power for life. That power is not
explained, it is only witnessed to. It is linked to faith and
to prayer, to a refusal to accept the widow's little faith
or the king's little power. The world enacted by Elijah
breaks all such conventions, routines, and stereotypes:
New news has come. The boy lives! The news given us in
this story is that the power for life is offered. It is carried
by a human agent.

This is Lent. We are in a season on the way to new life,
but now it is time for passion, suffering, death, denial,
repentance. In our Lent we yearn for Easter. In our
deathliness, we wonder about the gift of life. Our question is the same question asked by Elijah and the widowed
mother. It is the question of life. How is life possible
among us in our massive, resistant defeats? How is life
possible?

Two things come clear in this story about Lent.

First, the power for life in the face of our deathliness

is urgent. We are surrounded by fallen sons and hopeless widows. We yearn to have that power to transform life.

Second, that power for life is probably not available when we eat too well in the presence of the king. Elijah's power comes along with his eating habits.

Lent is a time to think about another diet, another nourishment, another loyalty. In various ways, we are all seduced, domesticated, and bought off—economically, religiously, intellectually, politically, morally. It is the story of our life. Bought-off people never have power for life.

The Lenten agenda for us all is this: Is it possible to do what the king cannot do? Life is indeed offered. But it is not given cheaply or at random. It is not given the way the world would dispense such power. No wonder the woman was amazed. Life has to do with sons given back, with daughters restored, with energy and courage granted, with hope and joy and well-being made new for us. Life is promised to the ones who eat thin and pray hard. Life is given by God. Power is granted to do what the king can never do.

> *In this season of Lent, teach us again the source*
> *of true power for life. Feed us with spiritual food*
> *that will fill us with energy, courage, freedom, and*
> *authority that we may be your agents of healing in*
> *the world. Amen.*

New Song, New Reality

I will lay waste mountains and hills,
     and dry up all their herbage;
I will turn the rivers into islands,
     and dry up the pools.
I will lead the blind
     by a road they do not know,
by paths they have not known
     I will guide them.
I will turn the darkness before them into light,
     the rough places into level ground.
These are the things I will do,
     and I will not forsake them.
                              —Isaiah 42:15–16

C an you imagine writing this poem and singing this
song in exile? Can you imagine defying the empire by
sketching out this daring alternative? Can you dare to sing
this song, under the very nose of Babylonian soldiers, about
a new reality that counters the empire? Think of it: new
reality conjured in worship, by the choir, inviting to new
courage, new faith, new energy, new obedience, new joy.

You see, the song is as subversive as is the new reality.
The new song never describes the world the way it is now.
The new song imagines how the world will be in God's
good time to come. The new song is a protest against the
way the world is now. The new song is refusal to accept
the present world as it is, a refusal to believe this is right

or that the present will last. The church is always at its most daring and risking and dangerous and free when it sings a new song. Because then it sings that the power of the gospel will not let the world finally stay as it is.

So here we are, in our society, with little energy, less courage, and diminished influence . . . I think we are not unlike those ancient exiles, scattered where we do not have much impact, sensing that the world is resistant to change, aware that the policies and practices all around us are aimed at death. We are close to despair in our weakness and futility.

About many things it appears that not much can be done. When this community of faith could do very little, however, it did not resign itself to playing it safe. Instead, it sang new songs, counter songs that refused to let the promise of the gospel sink into the landscape of the empire. The new song is a protest. The new song is also a bold assertion, innocently declaring that the God of the gospel has plans and purposes and a will to reorder the world, to bring wholeness and health to the blind, the poor, the needy, the nations so fearful, and the entire creation now so under killing assault. The song asserts God's good will against the deathliness. The song asserts God's future against our present tense. The song asserts God's relentless faithfulness in the midst of our desperate fickleness.

> *In the midst of exile, we look for you, O God.*
> *Teach us your new song that we may present a*
> *counter to the ways of death and celebrate your*
> *faithfulness and the new life that you are ever*
> *bringing into being. Amen.*

The Snares of Death and the Drama of Good News

> Then they told what had happened on the road,
> and how he had been made known to them in the
> breaking of the bread.
>
> —Luke 24:35

D id you know that the classic Reformation sermon had three accent points? The three points that shaped the classic evangelical sermon were three crucial theological claims:

- that we are caught in the snares of death;
- that we have been rescued by the power of God;
- that we are released to a new life of gratitude.

That is the sum of the Gospel. And we can, if we are not vigilant, default on any of these three claims:

- We can *refuse* to recognize that we are caught in the snares of death.
- We can *deny* the saving power of God who changes everything.
- We can *reject* a new life of gratitude.

But the accent for us is not on our possible refusal or our possible denial or our possible rejection. It is, rather, on our willingness to walk through this drama that, because of the goodness of God, keeps being reperformed again and again, in the life of the world. We baptized people are witnesses to the claim that this drama is real and valid and transformative.

We can be on our way with new life and new energy, and new noticing about the need in the world and the resources for healing, seeing now that old enemies are really needy neighbors, seeing that what looked like scarcity is enough when shared, enough to feed a crowd when there is gratitude. And we find that we are less greedy, less anxious, less coercive, less self-preoccupied, because we are able to rest our lives and our bodies down in the bottomless goodness of God. We come at the neighborhood with glad hearts and open hands and risk-taking lives, because the deep deathliness in our own lives has been overcome.

It turns out, it's not just three points. It is the truth of our lives. And now it is on offer, again, today, for us. It turns out that the snares are powerless; they are overrun by waves of gratitude that has us on our way rejoicing.

> *Lord, meet us once again at the tables of our lives.*
> *Command us once again to love as you have loved*
> *us. Empower us once again to live the story. Amen.*

A Way other than Our Own

For my thoughts are not your thoughts,
   nor are your ways my ways, says the LORD.
For as the heavens are higher than the earth,
   so are my ways higher than your ways
   and my thoughts than your thoughts.
                              —Isaiah 55:8–9

These words were uttered, first of all, to our community of faith in exile, when Israel was in deep need and in deep servitude to the Babylonian empire. There was cause for despair, a sense that there was no way out of exile, for Israel had tried every way it could think of, and all those ways had failed. And now, says the poet, there is another way. It is not your way. You would not have imagined this alternative way nor been able to predict it, and you surely cannot control it. There is a way into the future in your life, because God is at work doing strange, wondrous things for you and in spite of you, and your job is to get your mind off your ways of need and control, to give your life over to God's large, hidden way in your life.

In my judgment, the church in the United States must now face hard decisions such as we have not faced for a long time. We have indeed bought in as individual persons, even as a church, on consumerism, aimed at self-indulgence, comfort, security, and safety. We live our lives out of our affluence, and we discover that all our self-indulgence makes us satiated but neither happy nor safe.

This U.S. propensity, moreover, is supported by militarism, by strength, muscle, and intimidation, so that our culture, its images and its rhetoric, is saturated with military pictures bespeaking violence and brutality, and none of it makes us safe. It is like being taken in by the values of the Babylonian empire, with its lush dreams of war and promises of prosperity.

But none of that is for Israel, so says the poet. None of it is for the church. None of it is our proper way in the world. So the poet holds out to the exiles (and to us) an alternative way, the waters of baptism, the bread of the Eucharist, the wine of new covenant, the capacity to risk and trust and obey, and then to find ourselves safe and joyous, close to God, and enlisted for a very different life in the world.

> *God of homecoming, be with us as we journey*
> *through Lent. May we learn to relinquish our old*
> *ways so that we are ready to receive your newness.*
> *Amen.*

Boundary-Crossing Generosity

> . . . if you confess with your lips that Jesus is Lord
> and believe in your heart that God raised him
> from the dead, you will be saved.
>
> —Romans 10:9

Paul makes an argument about the prerequisites of faith that we may ponder in Lent. Here there are only two such prerequisites for following Jesus:

First, confess that *Jesus is Lord*. Do that with your lips. Believe that in your heart. That does not include all the authoritarian baggage we have accumulated in our several church traditions. Only the claim that Jesus, not the emperor, not the system, not our class or our nation state, can claim our loyalty. It's hard, but it is not complicated.

Second, affirm that *God raised Jesus from the dead*. Lent is on the way to Easter. There is no discussion here about whether it is a physical or spiritual resurrection, about historical realism or metaphor. Simply the lean claim that the executioners did not and could not keep him dead. Because God, that deep power for life, has shattered the system of death and made all things new. The Easter claim is not simply about resuscitation but about a new reality in the world that is unrestrained by the force of fear or violence or privilege. Paul must become lyrical about this claim, because the reality outruns all of our explanations. And we may situate our lives in this most elemental claim of the living Lord who opens new reality to us.

From that Easter claim Paul draws a deep and decisive conviction upon which everything is based: the Lord is the Lord of all and is *generous to all who call upon him.* The defining mark of the Easter world is *divine, cosmic generosity* that outruns our need and our want and our hope and our desire, to endow us with every good gift, most wondrously the gift of new possibility.

There is no class structure. There is no exceptional tenure or entitlement, no riding in the back of the bus, no exclusion of Gentiles—women, or conservatives, or progressives, or gays, or whomever we fear and want to exclude.

God is bringing the world to a new inclusiveness on the basis of God's own generosity. And God is now calling the church to engage that inclusiveness, because all of our preferred distinctions are vetoed at Easter.

> *Deep Power of Life, draw us into your boundary-crossing generosity. May we be on the way toward others, toward new life, in sync with the one who is Lord of Easter. Amen.*

The Future

"As for me, this is my covenant with you: You
shall be the ancestor of a multitude of nations.
No longer shall your name be Abram, but your
name shall be Abraham; for I have made you the
ancestor of a multitude of nations. I will make
you exceedingly fruitful; and I will make nations
of you, and kings shall come from you."
                                        —Genesis 17:4–6

The long history of faith, with all the saints, is the
story of walking into the future given by God. Lent
is a time for sorting this out. Popular Lent is too much
preoccupied with guilt and repentance. But not here.
Lent is rather seeing how to take steps into God's future
so that we are no longer defined by what is past and no
longer distracted by what we have treasured or feared
about the present. Lent is for embracing the baby given to
old people; resurrection to new life in Easter; and the offer
of a new world made by God from nothing.

If you want verification that God's promises are
kept, you will not find that verification among the new
atheists who have reduced everything to a tight little
package of reasonableness that easily explains everything away. Nor will we find verification among the
fundamentalists who have God in such a box that there
can be no room for inexplicable gifts. You will find verification among the daily performances of the trusting

46

ones who live out their trust in ways that the world terms foolish:

- in a church ready to be venturesome into God's future;
- in a church that pays attention to those disqualified by the capitalist system;
- in the acceptance of those who are unacceptable;
- in the commitment of time to neighbors when we prefer to have that time for ourselves;
- in the telling of hard truth about the world, and that in a culture of denial;
- in the slant toward justice and peacemaking in a world that loves violence and exploitation too much;
- in footing the bill for neighborliness and mercy when we have many other bills to pay;
- in lives that give testimony before the authorities who want to silence and intimidate and render others irrelevant.

It turns out that the world teems with verification, concerning babies from the barren ones, lives that have surged in the midst of death, hurts that have been healed, estrangements that have been reconciled, enslavements that have turned to freedom: all around us, particular, concrete, specific, for people like us.

So imagine, in this Lenten season, moving beyond treasured pasts, moving beyond precious present tense arrangements to new God-given prospects.

> *God, you are the one who gives us a future,*
> *who shatters our categories with extravagant*
> *generosity. Make us ready to receive this Lenten*
> *season. Amen.*

The Dangerous State of Blessedness

Then he looked up at his disciples and said:
"Blessed are you who are poor,
    for yours is the kingdom of God."
—Luke 6:20

Jesus intends that his disciples—his church—should be blessed. The church should be "lucky" people. He used the term "blessed," which means utterly satisfied, at peace, in joy. The word is used in its extreme form for the birth of a baby. That is the true blessed event when everyone is relieved, safe, full of joy and expectation, because the world seems innocent and we begin again. That is the kind of well-being Jesus intends for his disciples.

But Jesus' notion of blessed is a demanding one; his comments are in a tone of instruction and obedience. He requires that the disciples have a completely different *take on the present*:

- blessed are you poor;
- blessed are you who are hungry;
- blessed are you who weep now;
- blessed are you when people hate you and exclude you and defame you.

These are hard sayings to the church. Blessed is the church that does not easily come to terms with the present, that keeps loose and open enough, restless enough to know that the present arrangements of reality are not good enough, and they are not the way God intends them.

If you take that list of poor, hungry, weeping, hated, it means that the church is to be odd in the world, noticed in the community for walking to a different drummer. What Jesus intends is that the church should share in *the suffering of Jesus*, the Good Friday suffering of Jesus, because Jesus' way in the world is not popular or safe.

Jesus counters the blessed with the opposite word "woe," which means "big trouble." The extreme case of woe is death, sadness, failure, defeat. And so he says "woe" four times about those who have come easily to terms with the present:

- woe to those who are rich;
- woe to those who are full now;
- woe to those who are laughing now;
- woe to those of whom all speak well.

Woe—trouble—to those who have settled in on the present tense as though this were the end and culmination of everything, who are satisfied, comfortable, at ease, accommodating, without the alertness and the critique of the suffering of Jesus.

Christians are blessed when they maintain an awareness and a *practice of the present*, remembering that this present is not how God wills it.

> *God of discontent, you are not satisfied with the present state of the world—and you expect us not to be satisfied with it either. Teach us to identify with the suffering of Jesus in this world and so to live into the blessing you desire for us and for all. Amen.*

Scarcity and Plenty

> Taking the five loaves and the two fish, he looked
> up to heaven, and blessed and broke the loaves,
> and gave them to his disciples to set before the
> people; and he divided the two fish among them
> all. And all ate and were filled.
>
> —Mark 6:41–42

We have this wondrous story of Jesus transforming the wilderness into a place of nourishing plenty. Jesus radically disrupts how the world was thought to be. The wilderness, the "deserted place" in the story, was where there was no viable life-support system. He thought he was going there to rest, but he was met by a big crowd of those who were drawn to him. They believed he would indeed disrupt their failed world, though they knew not how.

Jesus did not disappoint them. He was moved with great compassion when he saw the hungry crowd. He had his stomach turned by their need. He engaged their hunger, because they lived in a false world without resources. His disciples accepted the barren wilderness without resources as a given; they wanted the crowd dispersed. They tried to protect Jesus from the need of the world. But Jesus scolded them and told them to feed the crowd. But they were without resources. They said, "We do not have resources to do that," only puny supplies of bread and fish. They accepted the scarcity and force of the wilderness. The crowd may have expected food, but his

50

disciples have no such hope. They have no such hope, even though they have traveled with Jesus and watched him work.

The story we tell about scarcity is a fantasy. It is not a true story. It is a story invented by those who have too much to justify getting more. It is a story accepted by those who have nothing in order to explain why they have nothing. That story is not true, because the world belongs to God and God is the creator of the abundant life.

All of us are invited to be children and practitioners of this other story. We act it out in ways that disrupt our society, even as Jesus continues to disrupt our world of scarcity with his abundance.

> *We are constricted by stories of scarcity. Break through these false tales with the surprising truth of abundance. May we bask in your shalom and then perform your story of generosity over and over again. Amen.*

Pain That Transforms

Why do you cry out over your hurt?
    Your pain is incurable.
Because your guilt is great,
    because your sins are so numerous,
    I have done these things to you.
Therefore all who devour you shall be
      devoured,
    and all your foes, every one of them, shall go
      into captivity;
those who plunder you shall be plundered,
    and all who prey on you I will make a prey.
                   —Jeremiah 30:15–16

Israel keeps telling the same story over and over. It is the story of going into pain and coming out in joy. It is the story of facing loss and receiving a gift. Most especially it is, in the Old Testament, the story of losing home in sadness and coming home to well-being. When that story gets retold by the church, it is the story of a Friday death and a Sunday miracle of new life. That story attracts us and claims our attention because when we are thoughtful and self-aware, we recognize it as the story of our life in the world. Personally and socially we do the story over and over, moving into death and out into new life. And the church is the place where we engage that story, because the world is too busy for it or too cynical or too anxious or too much in denial.

This is a remarkable poem that we claim as revelation. The poem reveals the thickness, the depth, the contradiction, the torment of God's own hurt over a city that God loves but can hardly tolerate. It is like that with a teenager . . . love but hardly tolerate. It is not true that love always wins. But love wins in this poem, and that is enough disclosure for this day. The disclosure is that God runs through *alienation*, into the silence of *pain*, and on to healing *newness*. That is the story of the day. That is the story of Jerusalem in Jeremiah, of defeat, displacement, and restoration. That is the story of Jesus, of Friday abandonment, Saturday depth, and Sunday readiness. It is the story that lets us read our own story afresh.

The burden of a poet is not explanation, because explanations never satisfy or convince. Rather the burden of a poet is to disclose, to reveal, so show what has not been seen or said until that instant. What is shown here to us is that there is a season of loss not to be avoided, a hope beyond, and a deep time of brooding between.

> *God of transformation, be with us in our loss,*
> *our brooding, and our hope. May we linger in*
> *faithfulness, not denying our pain nor cutting*
> *short our brooding. May we resist facile hopes; may*
> *we wait for you. Amen.*

Hope from Memory

For a brief moment I abandoned you,
  but with great compassion I will gather you.
In overflowing wrath for a moment
  I hid my face from you,
but with everlasting love I will have compassion
    on you,
    says the LORD, your Redeemer.

This is like the days of Noah to me:
  just as I swore that the waters of Noah
  would never again go over the earth,
so I have sworn that I will not be angry with you
  and will not rebuke you.

—Isaiah 54:7–9

Troubled times can drive one back into one's memory, hoping there to find reassurance or stability. The person who tries to go back there, however, immediately is on an imaginative shuttle, moving many times quickly back and forth between then and now; present trouble and old memory impinge on each other in odd and unexpected ways, present and past each illuminating and reshaping the other.

Ours is a time like the flood, like the exile, when the certitudes abandon us, the old reliabilities have become unsure, and "things fall apart." The falling part is happening for conservatives, and it is happening for liberals. It is happening all around us and to all of us.

In such a context of enormous fearfulness, our propensity is to enormous destruction. We grow more strident, more fearful, more anxious, more greedy for our own way, more despairing, and, consequently, more brutal. That propensity to destructiveness is all around us. On many days we succumb to its power; we succumb to the need to look only after ourselves and our kind, only selfishly, only ideologically, only "realistically."

The alternative is an act of imagination seeded by memory, uttered by a poet that draws the health-giving memory into the present, so that the present is radically reconstituted. Such an act of imagination is not shaved down to fit our realism, to conform to our interest, or to accommodate our conventional reality. We do not need poetry or artistry or imagination, if we only want to wallow in our status quo. The poet stakes a claim against such present reality. This act of imagination subverts our status quo and invites us to an alternative.

The world comes at us in destructive, pathological ways. From out of the chaos, however, emerges this other voice rooted in memory and comes the text shaping our future not in hostility but in compassion, not in abandonment but in solidarity, not in isolation but in covenant, not in estrangement but in well-being.

In the midst of troubled times, be with us, God of well-being. May faithful remembering lead to compassionate reimagining. Amen.

God of the Gnats

Then the LORD said to Moses, "Say to Aaron, 'Stretch out your staff and strike the dust of the earth, so that it may become gnats throughout the whole land of Egypt.'" And they did so; Aaron stretched out his hand with his staff and struck the dust of the earth, and gnats came on humans and animals alike; all the dust of the earth turned into gnats throughout the whole land of Egypt. The magicians tried to produce gnats by their secret arts, but they could not. There were gnats on both humans and animals.

—Exodus 8:16–18

You might think this is a very odd text with a very primitive plot that is remote from us. Except that Jews and Christians have been reading this text for a very long time. And every time we read it, we find it remarkably contemporary. We find it contemporary because we know that the characters are still active in the world:

There is *still pharaoh*, a king of absolutism, perhaps it is a military-economic-political leader, perhaps a nagging moralism, perhaps a closed-down sense of self, or a failed family with eating disorders, or an empty, bereft community exhausted in anxiety.

There are *still the magicians* of the empire, those who lack critical edge and use their gifts only to serve in blind, thoughtless ways the ideology of control and certitude.

There are *still those who stand free alongside Aaron and Moses*, who know that there is an alternative that arises underneath the absolutism. They are the ones who create space and energy and possibility for life outside the coercive system.

And the news that I declare to you is that YHWH, the Lord of creation and the *God of the gnats, is still on the loose*, declaring possibilities out beyond pharaoh, asserting that we do not need to submit to the force of empire, whether it is military and economic, religious and moral, or whatever. We may stand with this slave community, grinning and dancing and leaving, finding space for freedom and *shalom*.

We are not called to aid and abet the pharaohs that loom in our lives. We are called, rather, to depart, to trust the new life, and to find space and energy for a life of full *shalom*, to live apart from the system of pharaoh. This story has many futures. It turns up all through the Bible and all through the life of faith. The news is that the story still echoes in our lives, against all the powers of death. The gospel is always an offer of "gnats to you," gnats as signs of freedom for a different life. The power of death stinks in its decay. And we owe it nothing more!

> *God of the gnats, soften our hearts. May we turn from the ways of death and turn toward your shalom. Amen.*

Like Eagles Renewed

But those who wait for the LORD shall renew
   their strength,
   they shall mount up with wings like eagles,
they shall run and not be weary,
   they shall walk and not faint.
                              —Isaiah 40:31

Here is the good news. The good news is that we need not serve the wrong god, trust the wrong life-giver, fear the wrong power. We may read life differently, and the way to do that is to wait: to wait in eager longing for the God of creation and rescue to work a new way in the world; to wait in keen expectation; to wait in active zeal, receiving every hint of newness and acting on it; to be ready to go for the gift of life; to leave off fear, intimidation, resignation, pooped out-ness as the governance works a newness.

This poetic utterance about God and God's work has concrete counterparts in the realities of economics, politics, social relations, social possibilities. The utterance is matched by a reordering of reality, the transfiguration of the empire itself.

It is such an intellectual travesty, such an act of chutzpah, such a subversive poetic utterance that dumps a poem in the midst of resignation. The poem works a newness, not because it is good poetry, but because the subject of the poem, the God who lives in and through and with and under such outrageous assertion, is at work overriding despair, inviting hope, responding to our waiting, and starting the world free again, outside the regimes of weariness. We are left to decide about this outrageous assertion, sung against the resignation of the empire.

I happen to think this poem and its claim come very close to our reality, very close to our succumbed humanity, very near to the empires of deathliness—political, economic, intellectual—that wait immobilized in fear and docility. Citizens of the empire run the rat race and end up as frightened, defeated rats. The key religious question among us is whether there is grounds for an alternative, an alternative rooted not in self-preoccupation or in deadening stability but rooted in a more awesome reality that lives underneath empires, that comes among us as odd as a poem, as inscrutable as power, as dangerous as new life, as fragile as waiting. The poet names the name and imagines new life, like eagles flying, running, walking.

> *Teach us, O God, to wait in eager anticipation of your salvation. In this waiting, may we discover the promised blessings of new strength, new courage, new freedom, and new life. Amen.*

Known, Named, and Unafraid

> But now thus says the LORD,
> he who created you, O Jacob,
>   he who formed you, O Israel:
> Do not fear, for I have redeemed you;
>   I have called you by name, you are mine.
>   —Isaiah 43:1

B eing unafraid is an odd vocation; but it is the vocation of all those who have been baptized. We are different when baptized. The Acts account of the early church says that the Spirit of God came upon the ones baptized, even as the Spirit came upon Jesus in baptism. A lot of silliness is taught about the spirit coming in baptism. But what the Spirit does is visit our lives—our persons, our bodies, our imagination, our money—with the freedom of God, so that we are unafraid in the world, able to live differently, not needing to control, not needing to dominate, not needing to accumulate, not driven by anxiety. The book of Acts is the study of the baptized, the ones the Spirit visits, the ones who are unafraid in the world. It says of that community of known, named, and unafraid people, "They turned the world upside down" (Acts 17:6). Or better to say, they turned the world right side up.

The truth is that frightened people will never turn the world, because they use too much energy on protection of self. It is the vocation of the baptized, the known and named and unafraid, to make the world whole:

- *The unafraid* are open to the neighbor, while the frightened are defending themselves from the neighbor.
- *The unafraid* are generous in the community, while the frightened, in their anxiety, must keep and store and accumulate, to make themselves safe.
- *The unafraid* commit acts of compassion and mercy, while the frightened do not notice those in need.
- *The unafraid* are committed to justice for the weak and the poor, while the frightened see them only as threats.
- *The unafraid* pray in the morning, care through the day, and rejoice at night in thanks and praise, while the frightened are endlessly restless and dissatisfied.

So dear people, each of you: Do not fear! I have called you by name; you are mine!

> *In a world of fear and anxiety, you empower us to live lives of wholeness, lives that make the world whole and turn it right side up. Embolden us as those who know that they are called by your name. Amen.*

Fifth Friday of Lent

A Demanding
Long-Term Miracle

Then Abraham fell on his face and laughed, and
said to himself, "Can a child be born to a man
who is a hundred years old? Can Sarah, who is
ninety years old, bear a child?"

—Genesis 17:17

There is a dialogue set up in our faith. One voice says,
"Can you imagine!" The other voice answers, "Yes,
but." Abraham, old, almost cynical Abraham was filled
with "Yes, but." Yes, but I am very old. Yes, but she is
not pregnant. Yes, but we only have Ishmael. It is the
naked voice of the gospel that counters his tiredness. Can
you imagine a new son born right then? Can you imagine
a covenant kept to countless generations to come? Can
you imagine land given to landless people? Not: can you
implement it, can you plan it, can you achieve it?—only:
can you entrust possibilities to God that go beyond your
own capacity for control and fabrication?

God brings into existence that which does not exist.
Did you know that the Bible never uses the word *create*
with a human subject? We may "make" or "form" or "fab-
ricate," but only God creates, only God works a genuine
new possibility, a new thing beyond our expectations and
our extrapolations. It belongs to the mystery and holiness
of God to call to be that which is not yet. Because this is
God's world, the world is not closed, either by our hopes
or by our fears.

62

Those of us who gather around these texts and these powerful memories keep alive in our lives the terrible, unsettling transaction between "Yes, but" and "Can you imagine?" Most of the time, "Yes, but" wins. But by God's powerful grace, the "Yes, but" of our resistance is broken. Newness appears; we can sing songs, unembarrassed, songs about miracles.

No one could have foreseen how long-term and how demanding was the birth of Isaac. That single birth is long-term even until now. It is demanding because its newness requires many relinquishments—economic, intellectual, religious, political. It requires especially relinquishing that "Yes, but" that hinders our singing. What it demands, however, is more than matched by what it gives—newness, things that do not yet exist. We would not have thought that this birth would lead to such possibility and such demand. But then, Isaac is no ordinary miracle. And the God who birthed Isaac is no conventional God. This God intends us no conventional life.

> *Deliver us from the shackles of "Yes, but" and free us to sing songs of miracles. Open our hearts and minds to your creative word, which calls into being things that don't yet exist and brings life that is extraordinary and new. Amen.*

Re-formed by Jesus

> And all of us, with unveiled faces, seeing the
> glory of the Lord as though reflected in a mirror,
> are being transformed into the same image from
> one degree of glory to another; for this comes
> from the Lord, the Spirit.
>
> —2 Corinthians 3:18

P aul writes to the church in Corinth. It is, we know,
a troubled, struggling church, busy with "Christ
and culture" issues, many disputes of a quite practical
kind. Imagine ordinary people arguing about sexuality
and money and leadership and how to be faithful. Paul
cuts underneath all those disputes to remind these day-
to-day Christians that they are not ordinary people, but
they have at the core of their existence an implosion of
God's holiness that reshapes and redefines everything.
What counts finally is that the incursion of God's holiness touches our lives and our life together, or it does
not matter at all. I remind you, simply, of our oddness as
Christians that keeps us restless and hope-filled and alive
in the world, for the world.

Paul wants, first of all, to keep Christians at Corinth
connected to Jesus as the decisive point of their lives: "Such
is the confidence that we have through Christ toward
God. . . . all of us, with unveiled faces, seeing the glory of
the Lord" (2 Cor. 3:4, 18).

Paul makes a simple but crucial affirmation that it is

exactly in Jesus, only in the Lord, that the full holiness of God has touched down in human life. The point is so obvious and so easily forgotten. The church keeps its faith by remembering the decisiveness of Jesus.

The church at Corinth is not called to pious, romantic, goosey religion but simply to practice the memory of Jesus and to let that memory be fully present tense. When that story of Jesus is present tense, we are able to sort out and identify all the empty claims where God's holiness and God's power for life do not reside, where God's power for life is not embodied or enacted. Christians sort these matters out around Jesus, because we are endlessly seduced by imagining the glory is to be found in our technology, in our brightness, in our achievement, in our power, in our wealth, in our loveliness, or in our fitness. No, no, no! It is found in the face and body and life and story of the one who suffers in and with and for the world.

> *In Jesus Christ, your holiness has touched down in human life, remaking and reordering our values and expectations. Keep us restless and hope-filled and alive in the world, for the world. Amen.*

Until

If I had said, "I will talk on in this way,"
   I would have been untrue to the circle of
      your children.
But when I thought how to understand this,
   it seemed to me a wearisome task,
until I went into the sanctuary of God;
   then I perceived their end.
                                        —Psalm 73:15–17

But when he came to himself he said, "How many
of my father's hired hands have bread enough
and to spare, but here I am dying of hunger!"
                                        —Luke 15:17

It occurred to me that the Prodigal Son story is Jesus'
midrashic commentary on Psalm 73, in which the son
plays the role of the psalmist. The son is, "before," a prac-
titioner of commodity, saying:

> "'Father, give me the share of the property that will
> belong to me.' So he divided his property between
> them." (Luke 15:12b)

And he ends that scenario in a failed pursuit:

> "When he had spent everything, a severe famine
> took place throughout that country, and he began to
> be in need. So he went and hired himself out to one
> of the citizens of that country, who sent him to his

fields to feed the pigs. He would gladly have filled himself with the pods that the pigs were eating; and no one gave him anything." (Luke 15:14–16)

Then we are witnesses to his "after" when he returns home. But what interests us is the hidden turn of the narrative that is reported—like in Psalm 73—but, also like Psalm 73, not described: "But when he came to himself . . ." (v. 17).

What an incredible phrase! We do not know how that happened any more than we know how the "until" in the psalm worked. The teller of the story might have said, "Until he came to himself," because it is the same "until."

But, of course, the son does not just come "to himself." He comes to "himself" in his true identity. He comes to *himself as a beloved son* of the father. He in fact comes in his "until" to recognize that his father was the only one he wanted to be with. It did not matter anymore to this son that his older brother got the farm as his "portion," because the father is the son's "portion" and the only thing he wants in heaven or on earth. The son "coming to himself" is a decision grounded in the father's love that permits him to slough off his false self and become, finally, who he is. It is clear in this telling that Jesus fully understood the psalm. Indeed, Jesus' engagement in ministry is, among other things, that we should be weaned from the seductions of *commodity* for the gift of *communion*, a presence that leaves us in joy and well-being.

> *Bring us to our senses, O God. Turn our hearts away from the path of death and toward life, toward you, our true home, that we may ever live with joy in your presence as your people in this world. Amen.*

Called against the Distortion

> Consider your own call, brothers and sisters: not
> many of you were wise by human standards, not
> many were powerful, not many were of noble
> birth. But God chose what is foolish in the world
> to shame the wise; God chose what is weak in
> the world to shame the strong; God chose what
> is low and despised in the world, things that are
> not, to reduce to nothing things that are, so that
> no one might boast in the presence of God.
> —1 Corinthians 1:26–29

Jesus came to the Jerusalem temple, and he looked all
around. He came there because the temple is the cita-
del of meaning in that society, the symbolic expression
of all that is true and good and beautiful, the ultimate
hope and desire of his people for the presence of God. He
did not like what he saw: a totally distorted communica-
tions system that reflected a dysfunctional arrangement
of social power; the deep things of abiding value had been
cheapened and trivialized by greedy, exploitative practices. The core of faith had been coopted into aggressive
commodity transactions. Jesus acted decisively against
the distortion.

Imagine that God has called a people to live by the
commandments as an alternative to the distortion. Imagine that Jesus called his disciples to organize their lives
differently according to his teaching. Imagine that Jesus

has called the church to be a people in mission, the mission of subverting the dominant distortion of social reality. What an enormous call, to work as alternative to a social system gone crazy. It is an incredibly upstream vocation to live a different kind of life in order that the world may come to know that the pathologies in which we get caught are not the truth of our life.

The church has always been under call to live differently. Paul writes to the Corinthians: *Consider your call!* You are not just out there. You have been addressed, claimed, named, commissioned. You have been addressed in your baptism. Every time you take communion, you are called to the extravagant goodness of God, called to put your life down in the power and wonder of the creator God, called to remember that you are God's, that you belong to him and exist for him. Paul acknowledges that the ones called for God's work are not overly qualified for that work. "Not many of you," he writes, "are powerful." Not many of you are from noble families with good bloodlines. Not many of you are deeply valued by the powerful of the world. The call is to ordinary people who live ordinary lives.

People who depart the life of distortion find themselves floating in well-being, going back into the neighborhood in generosity, going to city hall with courage, living a true existence in response to the faithful gift of God.

> *You call us—ordinary people with ordinary
> lives—to be a church dedicated to your purposes,
> which are at odds with the values of the world.
> Strengthen us to leave behind all the distortions of
> life we indulge and to embrace the gift of wholeness
> and joy you have offered us in Christ Jesus. Amen.*

The Gift of a New Chance

No longer shall they teach one another, or say to
each other, "Know the LORD," for they shall all
know me, from the least of them to the greatest,
says the LORD; for I will forgive their iniquity,
and remember their sin no more.

—Jeremiah 31:34

What God has forgotten we no longer need remember. Our guilt, of course, lingers and haunts us and
slowly cripples us. Our sin is so serious because it violates
God. Now, however, God will no longer notice or credit,
and the sin will not linger or haunt or cripple. We shall be
free. There are libraries that have *book amnesties* in which
you can turn in old books without risk. There are communities with *gun amnesties* in which you can get rid of
unlawful guns. Until the amnesty, we must hide the book
or gun, and we cannot get rid of it. So it is with our bad
conscience, our moral failure, our sin before God. No
place to put it, no place to hide it, we cannot get rid of it.
And now a *general amnesty*. The power of guilt, fear, and
resentment evaporates, and we are free. What God has
unloaded, we no longer need carry as burden.

You see, the problem is that our actions toward each
other are so irreversible. We make a gesture, speak a word,
take an action. We may do it maliciously or carelessly.
In either case, that word or gesture or action generates
misunderstanding, distrust, hostility, alienation, and we

live with it forever and ever. There is no way out. Things grow more and more abrasive, until the alienations are deep and the hurt is beyond measure. I know families where a harsh word spoken forty years ago continues to alienate. Marriages stay frozen; parents and children are at deep odds. Among the nations, the great nations have so much for which to be forgiven by the little people, and the barbarity of race relations goes on and on in its poison. We ache for a chance to start again. But it costs so much—empty-handed, vulnerable, a vision of God's ready suffering for our freedom.

Jeremiah makes us pause for a moment before *the prospect of a new innocence*. Things need not go on and on. The cycle can be broken. A new chance is offered. Notice well, the new chance is demanding. It takes a broken heart, an end to self-sufficiency, abandoning a pretense of being right. This invitation, however, is not just advice on acting differently. This gospel is not advice but assurance. The assurance is that what we cannot do for ourselves is given us.

> *Forgiving God, we fall to our knees at the thought*
> *of a truly new beginning, a fresh start. Our*
> *hearts are broken, and we offer them to you in the*
> *assurance of your undeserved grace—the power*
> *that creates in us new hearts able to love. Amen.*

The Drama of Lent

The days are surely coming, says the LORD,
when I will make a new covenant with the house
of Israel and the house of Judah.
—Jeremiah 31:31

The core truth of our faith is this: the God of the gospel brings life out of death. We can line out the move from death to life physically, historically, literally, metaphorically, symbolically . . . any way you want. But the truth is a rock-bottom acknowledgment that God can probe into our deepest negations and create new possibility, new space for life, new energy for obedience, new waves of joy.

In the Christian tradition, the seal of the deal is Easter. On that dread Sunday morning the earliest church discovered that the Jesus who had been executed by the state was alive and on the loose; death had no power over God's will for life. The deathly systems of the empire had no grip on him even through his execution.

But in truth, the God of the gospel has been doing this forever.

It is this God of the gospel who took primordial *chaos* in hand, who said, "Let there be light" and formed a dry, ordered, fruitful land. And since that first moment, this God has been taking our dismal modes of chaos and forming them into launching pads for new life. That is life out of death!

It is this God of the gospel who came to that *barren*, hopeless couple Abraham and Sarah, in their old age, and gave them a child, an heir, and opened a future for them. And since then, the God of the gospel has been giving people futures when they thought there was no possibility for newness. That is life out of death!

It is this God of the gospel who came to the *slaves* in Egypt, weary of being cheap labor in a harsh production system. God heard their cry under exploitation, saw their abuse, and came down to deliver them. And since that awesome moment, this emancipatory God has been hearing the cries of exploited people and has been causing exploitative systems of cheap labor to collapse so that people can sing and dance in freedom. That is life out of death!

This is the drama of Lent, is it not? It is the journey of relinquishment of old visions of reality that are failed and being surprised by new life given in glad, inconvenient obedience. It is to this move that the God of the gospel invites us, again and again. This God is ready to give new life, more ready, as we say, to give than we are to receive.

> *You are the God who makes a way when there is*
> *no way. Free us from our anxious intransigence*
> *and our impoverished imaginations. Open us to*
> *your newness, the gospel gift given over and over*
> *and over again. Amen.*

Water and Vegetables

> And among them all, no one was found to com-
> pare with Daniel, Hananiah, Mishael, and Aza-
> riah; therefore they were stationed in the king's
> court. In every matter of wisdom and under-
> standing concerning which the king inquired of
> them, he found them ten times better than all the
> magicians and enchanters in his whole kingdom.
> —Daniel 1:19b–20

The story of Daniel is about Jews trying to maintain their acute faith identity in a complicated social environment where they had to deal with real worldly power. The king Nebuchadnezzar—symbol of complicated worldly power—recruits handsome, elite young Jewish boys for governmental service. They are put through a rigorous training program, socialized into the ways of the empire, educated, and wined and dined on the best food and drink the empire can pay for.

But Daniel was alert to his faith; because of his faith he resisted the rich food of the empire that would erode his Jewish identity. Indeed, says the text, it would "defile" him, compromise the purity of his faith. When he announced that he wasn't going to be eating such junk food, his supervisor said, "If you do that and then look poor, they will punish me for your failure to conform." But Daniel petitions him: "Let me try eating only vegetables and drinking only water for ten days, and see how I look."

Sure enough! At the end of ten days, Daniel looked better than all the rest of the members of the training program. And because there was then no risk to the supervisor, Daniel was permitted to eat only vegetables and to drink only water. The alternative was so good that his three Jewish friends in the training program did the same. They all were on a rigorous diet of faith.

At the end of the long training session, they had to appear before King Nebuchadnezzar to be examined, to be congratulated, and to be credentialed into a career in the empire. The king went down the line one cadet at a time, and he found that Daniel and his three Jewish friends were incomparably better than all the others, having lived according to their faith without any compromise. Daniel and his friends, under discipline, were the best recruits for high imperial service. They were able to accomplish that precisely because they did not compromise their faith. All the rest that follows of Daniel's service and influence in the empire is history—and no Jew who reads the story is at all surprised. Everyone in faith knows that the water and vegetables of faith produce well-being in the world of raw power.

> *Empower us, Lord, to resist the poor substitutes*
> *for true life on offer in our culture. May we not*
> *compromise with that which would weaken our*
> *faith. As we persevere on the journey, feed us with*
> *the bread of heaven that we may grow strong in*
> *you. Amen.*

A Secret World of Possibility

> Then turning to the disciples, Jesus said to them privately, "Blessed are the eyes that see what you see! For I tell you that many prophets and kings desired to see what you see, but did not see it, and to hear what you hear, but did not hear it."
> —Luke 10:23–24

We may go one step more with Jesus, if we ask finally what the disciples saw about Jesus that kings and prophets missed. The answer is the power of the cross. That is what this enigmatic statement of Jesus finally leads to, that everything true and powerful and transformative about Jesus comes into play in the cross. It is that Friday mystery that emerged when it appeared that the wise and the powerful, in the service of death, had committed capital punishment and eliminated from the world a terrible inconvenience. We learned only later that Friday, which seemed like defeat, turned out to be the good mystery of our future given by God.

In that hidden glimpse of Friday, we have learned all we need to know of God, for "no one knows who the Son is except the Father, or who the Father is except the Son and anyone to whom the Son chooses to reveal him" (Luke 10:22). We learn, in our way of confessing it, that Jesus is truly God, that God's power comes in weakness and vulnerability, that the power to transform is the truth of vulnerability, for the royal power of kings and the

76

majestic certitudes of the wise do not have the hidden, cunning power of healing.

More than that, we have learned—and keep needing to relearn—that the cross is not simply a one-time deal in the life of Jesus or of God. Rather the cross is the clue about how to live an alternative life in the world, an alternative life that is marked by risky innocence that has the power to heal, to create caring neighborhoods in the face of rapacious markets, to evoke new possibilities in the face of despair, to enact new forms of liberation in the face of endless locks of oppression. The clue, of course, is that none of this happens, unless there is a risk of self, so that the enhancement of the neighborhood requires the expenditure of self. But the babes and disciples have always known that, surely since that terrible, wondrous Friday.

Surely some of you are like me, preferring to be kings, prophets, wise, intelligent but all the while haunted by the secret world of costly grace that makes all things new. Lent is a good time to process that haunting, to inch over to the world of vulnerability, occupied by invisible horses of strength and chariots of newness.

Blessed are the eyes that see what you see!

> *God of the cross, your power is hidden in a*
> *weakness that quietly overcomes the world. Open*
> *our eyes to see this power at work. May we walk*
> *in it as we live out your alternative vision for the*
> *world. Amen.*

The Big Yes

[Moses] called the place Massah and Meribah,
because the Israelites quarreled and tested the
LORD, saying, "Is the LORD among us or not?"
—Exodus 17:7

This story puts Israel in the wilderness between slavery and the land of promise. Israel has a rich and embarrassing memory of the wilderness, about how Israel conducted itself in a time of danger and deficit. The theme of wilderness is an appropriate one for Lent, for Lent is about being in thin places without resources and being driven back to the elemental reality of God, the reliability of God, and our capacity to trust God in the thin places where there are no other resources.

What happens in this transaction is that the *water question* (material, concrete support for life) is turned into the *God question* concerning the one who "leads us beside still waters . . ." As a result, they dared to ask the question, "Is the Lord among us or not?" The Bible does not everywhere assume that God is present, but knows about the dry places where God's absence is overwhelming. They asked the God question about the water problem, because they knew they were up against it in their need and had no alternative.

And then quite tersely, God, with an assist from Moses, answers the anxiety of Israel. God hears the cries of Israel. God answers decisively. God gives water. God gives the water of life. And when God gives water for life, Israel's deep question is answered: Yes: the Lord is among us! Yes, God has the capacity to transpose wilderness into an arena for life. Yes, God is reliable. Yes, God is faithful. Yes, God is an adequate source for life in a context of scarcity and anxiety.

The story does not explain, any more than we explain Easter after Friday, well-being after Lent. And the reason we do not explain is that we are looking to God, the one who holds all circumstances and all emergencies, all possibilities and all needs and all gifts in God's own hand, the one who says "yes." The story is about God's inexplicable capacity to do well-being in a world that has been shut down. *Yes* even in wilderness, *yes* in Lent, *yes* from rock, *yes* to thirst. *Yes* to us, *yes* to the world, the story is about being dazzled beyond every explanation, *Yes, Yes, Yes!*

> *God of yes, you continually show yourself faithful.*
> *In the face of scarcity, in the barrenness of our*
> *wilderness places, you know our needs, and you*
> *meet them. All along our path, open our minds*
> *and hearts to trust you fully. Amen.*

In the Wrong Temple

> Jesus answered them, "Destroy this temple, and in three days I will raise it up." The Jews then said, "This temple has been under construction for forty-six years, and will you raise it up in three days?" But he was speaking of the temple of his body.
>
> —John 2:19–21

The Gospel of John likes to play tricks. For temple, *think Jesus*. For destroyed temple, *think Friday crucifixion*. For rebuilt temple, *think Easter resurrection*. So think of temple as the symbolic center of your life, as the place where you are met by the goodness and holiness of God, where you draw fresh on the core purpose of your life, where you get some clarity about who you are and what your life amounts to and how you will be remembered. And then think of duties and disciplines that belong to becoming fully whom you are called by God to be.

And then imagine, what if we are in the wrong temple, imagining our life in misguided ways and committed in the wrong directions? What if we are thinking temple-mall, theater, market, indulgence, when we should be thinking about Jesus and death and obedience and suffering and new life and joy?

In the wrong temple! The one where he came to clean things out and upset tables with a passion that seemed like violence: there is business and busyness and selling and trading and hoping to get ahead and buying access to God in the way you can buy it at the White House or in Congress, going there to be seen and valued and reassured. And then there is a sign, a deep gesture, a disturbance, an invitation that says, "You have got the wrong holy place, for the presence of God is not there."

The news is that this temple called Jesus is our true habitat. That is where we are bound in faith to live our life and put our buckets down and dream our dreams and claim our identities. Most of us, most of the time, find ourselves in the wrong temple, places that make promises of safety that leave us more anxious, offers of joy that leave us disconsolate. Partly we are in the wrong place by will, partly by habit, partly by accident, partly seduced. Our work in Lent is to move from these fake temples to the true temple who is Jesus. And then to receive a different life, the life he lives, the one to which we are invited.

> *Divine center of our lives, direct us toward the true temple that is our highest joy and deepest purpose—Jesus Christ. In this Lenten journey, may we ever more fully live in him and for him. Amen.*

On Changing Our Minds

Let each of you look not to your own interests,
but to the interests of others. Let the same mind
be in you that was in Christ Jesus,
who, though he was in the form of God,
did not regard equality with God
as something to be exploited,
but emptied himself,
taking the form of a slave,
being born in human likeness.
And being found in human form,
he humbled himself
and became obedient to the point of death—
even death on a cross.
—Philippians 2:4–8

Jesus made himself vulnerable in human form and became obedient. He became an obedient human person, and because of his passion for God's will for him, he collided with the will and purpose of the Roman Empire and with the Jews who colluded with the empire. He is not crucified because of some theory of the atonement. He is crucified because the empire cannot tolerate such a transformative, subversive force set loose in the world. Jesus' uncompromising commitment to the purpose of God contradicted the empire that lives against the grain of God's intention.

And Paul summons the church and its members to

exhibit in their common life the self-emptying that is congruent with Jesus. Paul knew about churches and about church people and the way we tend to act, concerned for self and our pet ideas and our intentions and our vested interests that bruise other people. And he said, do not look to your own interests.

So here is my bid to you for Holy Week. As we walk the walk from Palm Sunday to Easter through the Thursday arrest and the Friday execution and the long Saturday wait in the void, imagine all of us, in the wake of Jesus, changing our minds, renewing our minds, altering our opinions concerning self and neighbor and world. The clue to the new mind of Christ is emptying of our need to control and our anxious passion for security. And as our minds change, we come to new freedom. It is Easter freedom, unburdened and fearless, freed for the interest of the neighbor. So we worship this Jesus who was dead and is alive, who was humbled and is exalted. But we also replicate his life in our own life. We find ourselves with Easter liberty to be our true selves as he himself was his true self. We know this very well: 'tis a gift to be simple, 'tis a gift to be free, 'tis a gift to come down where we ought to be. And where we ought to be is right next to him in self-emptying obedience.

> *We are eager for Easter joy and new life, and yet we are haunted by the space between where we are and where you are. Grant us a new mind, a new readiness, a new heart, that we might stand with you in self-emptying obedience. Amen.*

An Alternative World at Hand

> May the God of hope fill you with all joy and
> peace in believing, so that you may abound in
> hope by the power of the Holy Spirit.
>
> —Romans 15:13

As Paul spoke of the *truthful reliability of God's promise*, he knew about a world of *fickle deception and betrayal*, as do we. The world of advertising, of ideology, of euphemism offers us endless phoniness that coerces and manipulates and invites into a virtual world that has no staying power.

Well, here is the news. Out beyond that fickle world there is the world of God's reliable fidelity, a God who makes and keeps promises, and you can dwell there.

As Paul speaks of the *God of hope* who gives new futures out of love, he knows about a *world of despair* that traffics in brutality. And so do we. The world of despair believes that there are no new gifts, no fresh generosity, no possibility of newness or forgiveness, and so life becomes a zero-sum game to see who can stay the longest on top of the heap, all the while knowing that there will be no good outcome to the futile rat race.

But here is the news. Out beyond that despair that sanctions road rage and violence against the poor and war and ruthless exploitation that leaves one exhausted if not half dead, there is an alternative world bodied in Jesus. It is a world of new gifts and fresh starts grounded in divine forgiveness and sustained by generosity. That world is on offer in this one who is about to be born among us.

As Paul envisioned *welcome of one another*, he knew about a *world of exclusion* that is grounded in fear and anxiety. And so do we. All around now are barriers and gates and fences that draw lines around gifts and possibilities and resources and access. The lines are drawn closer and closer until all are excluded except the blessed, cunning ones, and even they are left nervous about when the next wall will be built and who will then be excluded.

Here is the news. Out beyond the world of exclusion and rejection and hostility, there is on offer *a world of welcome* that sees the other not as threat or competitor but as cohort on the pilgrimage of humanity. That alternative world of welcome is signed by bread and by wine; but it is known by lives that reach out and touch in order to heal and transform.

> *God of all hope, we know all too well a world of*
> *betrayal, despair, exclusion, and conflict. May we*
> *live into your alternative world of truth, hope,*
> *welcome, and harmony as we trust and follow you.*
> *Amen.*

Drawn Away, Drawn Toward

"Now is the judgment of this world; now the
ruler of this world will be driven out. And I,
when I am lifted up from the earth, will draw all
people to myself."

—John 12:31–32

So here are three Lenten ponderings for us, as we stand
positioned between the ruler of this age in his seduction and the man of Nazareth who is the alternative:

1. The new truth of Jesus, honored by God, is that
   self-giving love is the wave of the future, and we are
   called to follow.
2. The Lord of the cosmos has signed on to this alternative we see in Jesus, because that is the very character of God.
3. The new way of suffering love in the world is a
   magnet that will draw us to new life.

Try this as a Lenten plot. Lent is the time we stand,
each of us—liberal and conservative—just between the
Lord of suffering love and the ruler of this world. We
stand there pulled in both directions and sense the enormous ambiguity of our life, wishing to care and be generous but wanting also to be selfish and have it our own
way. Lent is being drawn:

- to Jesus' way in the world, to Jesus' news, to Jesus' people who practice generosity and forgiveness and hospitality;
- away from the ruler of this world, away from greed, away from fear, away from anxiety, away from brutality.

We are all in this process. We are being *drawn toward*. We are being *drawn away*. The pivot point, the extreme case, is that Friday of forgiveness and thirst. But he said about himself and us, "Unless the grain of wheat falls into the ground and dies . . . it will not grow." The new growth from self-giving is Easter. Easter joy! Easter freedom! Easter goodness! But only via Friday. So we expect, in these thoughtful days, to be drawn to Jesus. Friday is his embodiment of self-giving love as a magnet. The heavenly God intends us to be attracted to it and therefore given a new start in neighborly community. Do not linger over the rulers of this world. They are being driven out. The text gives us the secret clue to newness. The world little suspects. But we know!

> *Draw us, Lord, toward you, toward your way of self-giving love. Draw us away from all that is not love—from the forces of greed, fear, anxiety, and brutality. In this Lenten experience of so being drawn toward you and away from the powers of the world, may we come to find that new life that is the meaning of Easter. Amen.*

Belonging and Washing

"So if I, your Lord and Teacher, have washed
your feet, you also ought to wash one another's
feet. For I have set you an example, that you also
should do as I have done to you."

—John 13:14–15

The disciples watched with indignation and astonishment, this Lord become a servant. As they watched, their anxiety ebbed some. And he said to them: "Do you know what I have done to you?"

The disciples are always concrete operational. They said, "Yes, you washed our feet."

More than that, he said. "So if I, your Lord and Teacher, have washed your feet, you also ought to wash one another's feet. For I have set you an example, that you also should do as I have done to you."

The drama of the towel provided an example for the disciples to replicate:

- Replicate the truth that you have come from God; you are not your own.
- Replicate the truth that you will go to God; your future is assured.
- Replicate that the space between you and others is filled with a towel.
- Replicate that as you travel with towel and basin, you will be safe in vulnerability, treasured in obedience, and free from anxiety.

Jesus offered an example to his disciples that was a sharp alternative to all the available models around him. He broke decisively with the model of control used by the Roman empire. He broke with the model of his religious context of stratification and purity. He broke with all the social realities that control and stratification produce and found himself free and traveling light.

In his great act of humility and washing, he broke with all the models of humanity that are visible in our own time and place: the rat race of productivity, the fear for survival, the frenzy of accumulation, and the deathly sense of self-sufficiency.

And then, to be sure we had not missed the point, he said to his disciples, "A new commandment I give to you, that you love one another; as I have loved you, that you also love one another. By that we will all know that you are my disciples if you have love for one another."

In this act, Jesus summoned and constituted an alternative community of which we are heirs. Imagine that a small community set down in the midst of the empire and all its aggressive militarism is a small community that refuses to participate in the anxiety of the world, because it imitates birds and lilies in the sure confidence that God in heaven knows our needs and supplies them.

> *In Jesus and his way of life, you have given us an example to replicate—an example that is in sharp contrast to the ways of the world. In the grace and power of your Spirit, may we be that community that refuses anxiety because of its sure confidence in you and so is empowered to reach out in compassion and love. Amen.*

Penultimate Honesty

I will praise the name of God with a song;
    I will magnify him with thanksgiving.
This will please the LORD more than an ox
    or a bull with horns and hoofs.
Let the oppressed see it and be glad;
    you who seek God, let your hearts revive.
For the LORD hears the needy,
    and does not despise his own that are in
      bonds.
                —Psalm 69:30–33

In the drama of Good Friday, only Jesus has a psalm for his use. We have no hint that either the governor or the crowd is allowed a psalm, that is, neither of them reaches into the old tradition for a guiding script on how to speak or what to say.

Psalm 69 shows how this counterpower of Jesus conducts itself, as though the political crudities of Rome and Jerusalem really do not count. I want to speak about the penultimate power of honesty. This is not the last word of the psalm, but it is the first important word. The psalm is something of an embarrassment to us, because we do not expect such speech, especially on the lips of Jesus. But Jesus is a child of this Jewish script. He knows that this is how the faithful speak in the face of such a crisis.

So what is it that happened in that drama of power on that Friday? Do not give up the question for a heavenly, transcendental transaction out beyond worldly reality, for these are real people struggling over real power. Friday is the ultimate day in which the church asks with unblinking honesty about the moral quality of reality. Or is it just that money talks and might makes right?

Jesus has become for us the lens through which we reread power, social relations, and formal policies. Jesus stands alongside all the powerless in his abrasive prayer, demanding justice on earth from God. Jesus' innocence is an exposé of and a threat to every other kind of power. It would indeed be quite an Easter if the church resolved to come clean on this moral claim. Talk about a coup! No wonder he made the governor nervous and the crowd frantic. They killed him, but he kept praying in his dangerous, abrasive honesty. The prayer he prays insists that God will not be mocked,

> "For the LORD hears the needy,
>   and does not despise his own that are in
>   bonds."
>
> v. 33

God of the poor and powerless, you have taught us how to speak in the face of inhumanity—you call us to tell the truth and expose the false orderings of power that oppress and kill. Make us bold to follow the example of Jesus and to speak your word, trusting in your justice and deliverance. Amen.

Expecting to Be Interrupted

Early on the first day of the week, while it was
still dark . . .

—John 20:1a

Nobody knew how long Saturday would last. Nobody knew if Saturday would ever end. So it is now as well. Nobody knows how long Saturday will last or if it will ever end. Saturday is that in-between day of stillness and doubt and despair when time stands still in lethal flatness. The old Saturday was about abandonment and disappointment at the far edge of the crucifixion. And then came all the Saturdays of fear and abusiveness, of the Crusades and the ovens and genocides in too many places. And then came our particular Saturdays of Katrina and 9/11 and economic collapse, Saturdays of overwhelming failure with no adequate resources.

In the midst of that desperate stillness, the church listens yet again to another narrative that interrupts and intrudes and summons and haunts. The key character of this other narrative around which we gather is the Friday guy done in by the rulers of this age. That much they knew on Saturday, but it did not comfort them at all on Saturday. The wonder of the narrative around which we gather is that the Friday guy did not linger long on Saturday. He ends up being the Sunday guy—not of good clothes and proper behavior and much piety but of the first day of the week . . . the first day of the new world,

92

and for those who engage, the first day of new life in the world.

This narrative about the Sunday guy is urgent among us because it is clear that the old narratives of money and power and violence and control have failed. There is among us a wonderment about another way in the world. This is it! It is discipleship after the guy who started the world again. And now in the church, all of us—conservatives and progressives—are wondering about this alternative.

We are not sure
But we expect to be interrupted.
We expect to be given a mandate.
We expect to be put at risk.
We are not sure; but we are haunted at the thought
    of it.

*You are the God who remains with us during our
Saturdays of waiting and wondering, marked by
the memory of Friday and the hope of Sunday.
Forbid us too-easy exits out of the darkness. May
we wait until we are at last interrupted by your
life-giving grace. Amen.*

Easter Sunday

Authorized for Risk

> When it was evening on that day, the first day
> of the week, and the doors of the house where
> the disciples had met were locked for fear of the
> Jews, Jesus came and stood among them and
> said, "Peace be with you."
>
> —John 20:19

While his followers met where the doors were
"locked for fear," he came. He stood there in
the midst of the violent restless empire, and he said,
"Peace be with you." They recognized him when they
saw the scars on his body, as he had been executed by
the empire. This was the same Jesus of whom they
despaired! And when they recognized him, he said a
second time, "Peace be with you." The story exhibits
the contradiction between the empire of death and the
Living One whom the empire could not keep dead. This
Easter Sunday we ponder that contradiction between
empire death and Easter life to consider our own faith
amid the empire and to be dazzled by the one who said
then and who says now, "Peace."

And then, "He breathed on them." In the Bible the
notion of "breath" is the same word as "spirit." He gave
them spirit. He performed artificial respiration on his
bedraggled followers. He said, "Receive the Holy Spirit,"
which is the spirit of Jesus. He gave them the surging
gift of surprising life, so unlike the lifeless charade of the

empire that only knows about violence and control but knows nothing about giving life.

Imagine a world of life come amid the destructiveness of empire. It is this life-carrier who said to his followers, "I give you the power to forgive sin." I recruit you for the forgiveness business. I charge you with healing, transformative reconciliation. It was then, and always is, a hard work for the church, because in the empire there is no free lunch, no open hand, no breaking of the vicious cycles of fear and violence and failure.

So here is my pitch. Imagine that you and I, today, are a part of the Easter movement of civil disobedience that contradicts the empire. Let's see what happens. Let's see if life is longer than death. Some will never move and will keep trusting in the empire. But we know this much: we have been breathed on. We have been addressed. To us he said, "Peace be with you." He said it three times, and then he charged us with forgiveness. We are on the receiving end of his offer of life . . . praise God!

> *You summon us to life in the midst of death, peace in the midst of violence, praise in the midst of despair. Filled once again with your unruly Spirit, may we answer your summons and be part of the movement of life. Amen.*

CPSIA information can be obtained
at www.ICGtesting.com
Printed in the USA
LVHW010556170121
676670LV00013B/116

9 780664 261696